IMAGES
of America

ROME REVISITED

Presidential candidate Theodore Roosevelt stands on the balcony of the Stanwix Hotel after scolding a small group of young hecklers. A large crowd turned out to hear this very charismatic person address the political and social issues of the day. (Rome Historical Society.)

On the cover: Please see page 65. (Author's collection.)

IMAGES
of *America*

ROME REVISITED

Peter M. Leonard

ARCADIA
PUBLISHING

Published by Arcadia Publishing
Charleston, South Carolina

Library of Congress Catalog Card Number: 2007931492

For all general information contact Arcadia Publishing at:
Telephone 843-853-2070
Fax 843-853-0044
E-mail sales@arcadiapublishing.com
For customer service and orders:
Toll-Free 1-888-313-2665

Visit us on the Internet at www.arcadiapublishing.com

*To the men, women, and children of Rome, past and present,
this work is dedicated to you all.*

CONTENTS

ACKNOWLEDGMENTS

When preparing a work of this nature it is impossible to acknowledge every single source of help that has been received over the years, and there have been many. Countless Romans have recalled tales of yesteryear to me, and I have been grateful to them for sharing them with me. I hope that I have chronicled a history of our city that is acceptable to all.

A special thank-you goes out to the following individuals for help with this specific project. David DeProspero of Reflections Photography aided me greatly in the photographic section of this work. Edwin Evans, a caretaker of Rome's history, has shared his time and knowledge with me over the years. John Parker provided some outstanding photographs for the Italian chapter of this book. "Grandpa" Paul Yager of the *Rome Observer*, a chronicler of Rome's history, helped insure the historical accuracy of this work and helped to identify the locations in many of the photographs. The Rome Historical Society provided research assistance and the use of a part of its photographic collections, hereby credited as RHS in the following pages. Special thanks also go to Tiffany Howe of Arcadia Publishing, for without her help and guidance there would be no book; Matthew Fidler, a history teacher with the Rome City School District, who really fostered my love for local history; my mother, Johanna, and sister Debbie for helping me with all the small projects from layout to editing; and my father, Peter Leonard, who was a Rome city fireman before his passing in 2003, for always encouraging me and spending time with me preserving the history of Rome.

INTRODUCTION

Looking at the city of Rome today, it is very hard to imagine that just 250 years ago this was all barren, thickly wooded forests. In the prehistoric period, glaciers covered most of New York. As the glaciers began melt, the running water carved out the features of the Mohawk Valley, leaving the land very fertile and suitable for farming. Paleo-Indians made their way into the area about 10,000 years ago and steadily flourished into what eventually became the Iroquois Confederacy. The Oneida Indians made their homes around Oneida Lake into the Wood Creek and the Mohawk River areas.

The first documented visit of the white man occurred in 1609. Six years later, in 1615, French military commander Samuel de Champlain led an attack against the Oneidas at their stronghold known as the Oneida Castle, and it was a disaster for the French. In the years following, Dutch fur traders moved into the Mohawk Valley and became allied with the Oneidas. In 1702, the royal governor of New York was petitioned to construct a road connecting Wood Creek and the Mohawk River. The petition was granted. The Oneidas called this portage the De-O-Wain-Sta, which literally translates to "the great carrying place." One would canoe down Wood Creek and would then have to carry their canoe a few miles to the Mohawk River.

In June 1755, Capt. William Williams of the 51st Regiment of Foot (British) was assigned to the Oneida Carry. Captain Williams was given an order that sealed the fate of this area forever and its due place in history. His men began to construct a fort, and once completed, he christened the new defense Fort Williams. The defense boasted four half-bastions and was situated on high ground on the banks of the Mohawk River. A French raid by Lt. Gaspard de Lery left Fort Bull in ruins and its garrison dead, including the commander Capt. William Bull. As a result, British major Charles Craven was sent to the Mohawk Valley to reinforce the defenses at the carry. Two new forts, Newport and Craven, were constructed, thus bringing the total to four defenses along the carry.

Fearing a massive French invasion via Fort Ontario, Gen. Daniel Webb was next sent to reinforce the Mohawk Valley. The western end of the carry had been left defenseless after Fort Bull was destroyed. A new defense bore the name of Fort Eagle. This fort also shows up on maps as Fort Wood Creek. It was a small stockade fort with a wet ditch on three sides and a pond on the fourth. Webb considered Fort Eagle a sturdy defense able to repel an attack of 500 enemy troops.

The British made the decision to build an extremely large fort at the carry. They were determined not to lose the carry again. In March 1758, Brig. Gen. John Stanwix was ordered to the carry and he took with him the 5,600 men of 60th Royal American Regiment based at Albany. The fort was completed by the summer of 1759. It was perfectly geometrical and not elongated, as often depicted in many early sketches of Rome. This design was important to gain accurate and destructive cross fires from all vantage points by the fort's garrison. The picket, sharpened vertical posts, and fraise, sharpened horizontal posts, were placed close together to prevent scaling ladders from being placed directly against the walls of the fort, thus allowing for an easy breach. A dry ditch added 10 feet of height to the massive wooden walls. Once in the ditch, an attacker would be vulnerable to musket and cannon fire.

In 1763, during the Pontiac Conspiracy, the fort was overhauled and a redoubt was added to its defenses. In 1768, Fort Stanwix was used as the meeting place for the Iroquois Confederacy and British Indian superintendent William Johnson. Here they signed the Boundary Line Treaty. The fort, which was crudely built, was in constant need of repair. The daily life at the fort was usually boring with little to do other than to survive in the wilderness. Occasionally they would help with the unloading of supply bateau.

In the summer of 1777, the garrison of the fort held off the British army during a 21-day siege. It was during this siege that the first Stars and Stripes flag was unfurled in battle. Three days later, a relief army of local militia and Oneida Indians were on their way to relieve the besieged garrison of the fort when they were ambushed on the hills of Oriskany. The militia commander Gen. Nicholas Herkimer, along with several Oneida clan leaders, was mortally wounded in battle. After several hours of fierce, bloody, hand-to-hand combat, a thunderstorm forced both sides to fall back. While the British army was fighting at Oriskany, the second in command at the fort, Lt. Col. Marinus Willett, led an attack on the British camps, seizing much-needed provisions, military correspondence, regimental colors, and a regimental drum, a first in American military history. The British were now without food and ammunition; combined with rumors of Gen. Benedict Arnold marching his way to the fort with a large contingent of Continental soldiers, they lifted the siege and fell back to Canada. Indirectly, by Fort Stanwix not surrendering, the British invasion of 1777 was thwarted, and combined with the surrender of the British army at Saratoga a few weeks later, the war was over in Upstate New York.

The actions of those brave defenders for 21 days is the pride and local spirit behind everything that has been accomplished in Rome throughout the years. Many products have bore the name Fort, Flag, or Fort Stanwix Brand to remind all of us about our Revolutionary heritage. Upon the ruins of that mighty fortress was built the city of Rome. The city grew to become a thriving metropolis that produced one-tenth of all copper-related products in the United States. It was here that the first shovel of dirt was turned to begin construction of the Erie Canal. It was here in the 1850s that the modern cheese-making process was perfected. Romans have fought in every major conflict since the Revolution and have amassed an impressive honor roll. Rome became home to Griffiss Air Force Base in the 1940s. Like the namesake in Italy, Italian Americans have left their indelible mark on the community. Sadly, as the world changed, Rome did as well. All of the major industries closed or relocated overseas. With the peace of the 1990s, Griffiss Air Force Base closed and Rome had to reinvent itself. Many strides have been made over the last decade to attract new prospects for the future, several of which have been the result of Rome hosting Woodstock in 1999.

One

IN THE BEGINNING

In the prehistoric period, large glaciers covered New York State. Erosion from the thawing of these glaciers created the Rome River, which carved out the features that made Rome a strategic area. The soil was very fertile, and portions of the Mohawk and Black Rivers along with Wood Creek made travel via water from Canada to the Atlantic Ocean possible. It was not until the mid-1600s that fur traders made their way into the Mohawk Valley and nicknamed this area the "Oneida Carry" or De-O-Wain-Sta, as it was known by the indigenous Oneida Indians.

On March 27, 1756, during the French and Indian War, a raid against British Fort Bull by the French left the entire garrison of men, women, and children massacred and the fort destroyed. The British army ordered Gen. John Stanwix and 5,600 soldiers to build a formidable defense at the carry in 1758. This stone marker at Fort Bull honors the memory of those massacred that day.

The first log laid was on August 26, 1758, and the fort was completed in 1759. By 1775, the fort was unmanned. Col. Peter Gansevoort and the 600 men of the 3rd New York Regiment took control of the fort in 1777. British colonel Barry St. Ledger led an attack against the fort in August 1777, with the sole purpose of recapturing the fort.

"I say that it is my determined resolution, with the forces under my command to defend this fort and garrison at every hazard, to the last extremity, in behalf of the United American States who have placed me here to defend it against all enemies," Col. Peter Gansevoort exclaimed to the British invaders demanding his surrender on August 3. Unhappy by the decision, St. Ledger laid siege to the fort.

An old photograph shows the remains of the battle flag carried throughout the Revolutionary War by Gansevoort's 3rd New York Regiment. This flag was the inspiration for the modern-day state flag.

In full sight of the British army, raised for the first time ever in battle, were the Stars and Stripes. August 3 holds a special place of honor for the citizens of Rome. Defiant for 21 days, the fort never surrendered and even received a mention in Congress for its bravery.

ORISKANY.
MONUMENT AND PANEL.
SHOWING GEN. HERKIMER DIRECTING
THE MOVEMENT OF HIS ARMY
AFTER BEING FATALLY WOUNDED.

Gen. Nicholas Herkimer mobilized the Tryon County Militia and began a 40-mile march to aid the defenders of the fort. Col. Barry St. Ledger ambushed Herkimer's army six miles from the fort on the hills of Oriskany. Several hours of fierce fighting forced both sides to withdraw with many casualties, including Herkimer. His men never reached the fort.

12

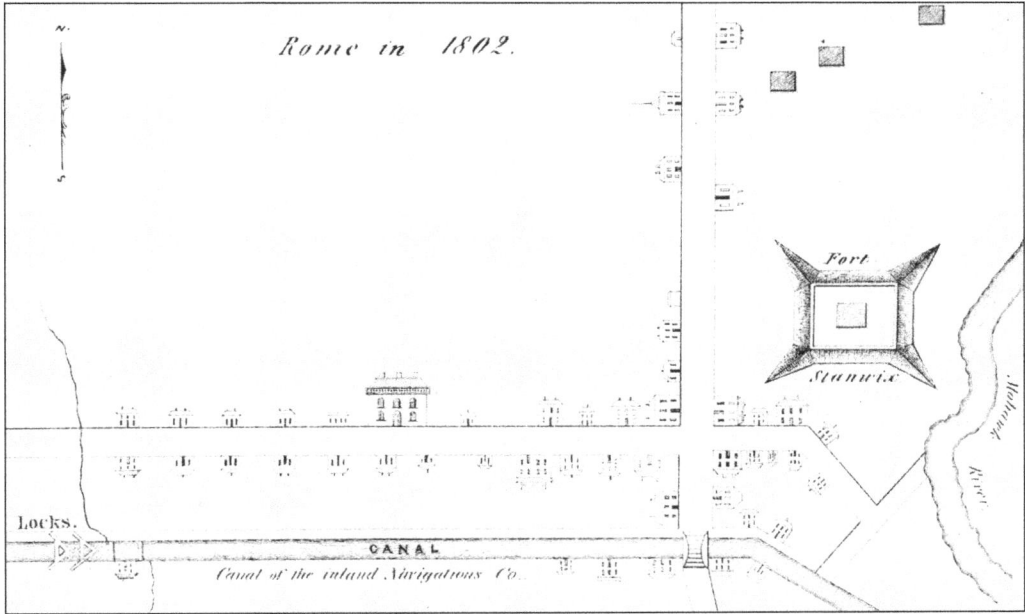

Rome in 1802.

In 1796, Dominick Lynch purchased the "Expense Lot," which became the heart of Rome. On his personal map of Lynchville there were only two streets, Dominick and James, named for his son. Unhappy with Lynchville, many early settlers decided on the name Rome in 1819, when the village was incorporated. In 1820, there were over 90 buildings and the population had increased to 3,000 people.

On July 4, 1817, to mark the beginning of the greatest engineering feat attempted in that time era, the Erie Canal, the first shovel of dirt was turned. The first completed navigable section of the Erie Canal was between Rome and Utica. The *Chief Engineer of Rome* made the maiden voyage in 1819 to much fanfare.

13

The 1817 Erie Canal skirted the outer limits of Rome. The widening and reengineering of the canal in 1844 redirected canal traffic through the center of Rome. As a result, hundreds of new businesses sprang up along the canal. The railroads would soon follow.

The Erie Canal ran east and west through New York, and the Black River Canal ran north and south with the southerly end emptying into the Erie Canal. Goods were shipped down the Black River from Boonville to Rome and then from there redistributed throughout the state via the Erie Canal.

Two

BIG BUSINESS
COMES TO TOWN

The Willett House, shown here before it burned in 1866, is symbolic of a new era in Rome. With the reengineering of the Erie Canal in 1844, hundreds of small businesses began to spring up, including major industry. Rome is centrally located in the geographic center of New York, and manufactured goods could easily be distributed anywhere in the state via the many canals or railways.

One of the earliest and largest manufacturing companies to open was the Rome Iron Works in 1866. After several reorganizations in 1891, it was renamed Rome Brass and Copper Company. By 1900, it employed well over 600 skilled workers, producing a wide assortment of copper wares.

Now occupied by St. John the Baptist Roman Catholic Church, the Rome Brass and Copper Company occupied a large part of East Dominick Street. Several consolidations and purchases eventually led to the formation of Revere Copper and Brass.

Almost every household in Rome used a teakettle from the Rome Manufacturing Company. At the plant on Railroad Street over 400 workers produced a full line of nickel-plated copper wares.

Revere Copper and Brass was the result of many consolidations of national manufacturing companies into one. It was here that two local chemists developed the process of fusing copper to stainless steel together. This led to the introduction of their world-famous line of Revere Ware cookware in 1939.

The Spargo brothers were the founders of the copper wire industry in Rome. After learning this trade in England, they arrived in Rome and opened the Electric Wire Works in 1883. Eventually James Spargo dissolved his partnership and started Spargo Wire on Railroad Street.

Like Revere, the General Cable Corporation was a consolidation of several smaller independent companies both locally and nationally. The Rome plant produced a large variety of electrical and magnetic wires. During World War II the factory converted to the wartime industry and was an important part of the war effort.

Using locally purchased copper, the workers of the Rome Turney Radiator Company located on Canal Street would then manufacture that copper into continuous hollow spiral tubing. This tubing became an essential product in the production of automobile and aircraft radiators, especially during the world wars.

Located at the far end of East Dominick Street was the massive 13-acre Rome Locomotive Works, which had roots dating back to the early 1880s. An estimated workforce of 500 constructed, repaired, and rebuilt hundreds of locomotive engines.

The Rome Grader Company, formerly part of the Rome Locomotive Works, produced a large variety of farm machinery. The Union Fork and Hoe Company was another local manufacturer of farm implements that bought their factory out. During World War II they were a major producer of bayonets for the military.

One of the cornerstone industries of Rome was Adams Foundry, which had its beginning back in 1835. This company played a major role in the city's industrialization. The foundry produced a broad range of products from steam engines to wheels, stoves, fences, and iron-based goods, as shown in its booth at the Greater Rome Exposition.

Workers pose in front of the Channel Steel Barge Company's "world's strongest barge." With a large public turnout on June 24, 1922, this barge was launched into the Barge Canal to begin service. The Barge Canal is the successor of the Erie Canal.

Pioneering the field of converting beets into refined brown and white sugars was the First New York Beet Sugar Company located on Doxtater Avenue. It was capable of processing over 200 tons of beets daily into the highest quality of sugars.

The Rome Soap Manufacturing Company's complex was located in the heart of East Dominick Street. Founded in 1856 by Charles Bradock, 3-B soap was a very well-known brand of soap in the early 20th century. It also manufactured a large line of high-grade textile, laundry, and household soaps. (RHS.)

The Selden Door and Sash Company local workshops on Front Street were absorbed into what became the Beach Lumber Company in 1897. The Beach Lumber Company continued in business for many years and acquired a very respectable reputation throughout the Northeast and Canada.

One of the premier grocery suppliers in Rome was the Ethridge family company, which had its early development in 1845. Before the beginning of the 20th century had arrived, the A. Ethridge Company was a leading wholesale manufacturer and distributor of canned goods throughout Upstate New York.

The textile industry in Rome was also a key source of employment. The Rome Steam Knitting Mills began to produce a full line of undergarments for the whole family in 1878. During the 1890s the name changed to the Williams Brothers Knitting Mill. Located on Henry Street, the mill had a workforce of 300 workers before closing in 1966.

The telephone came to Rome in 1876 when a Roman fashioned one together from plans based on a newspaper story of the new invention. The amount of users began to multiply exponentially, leading the Bell Telephone Company, the forerunner to AT&T, to establish an office in Rome. (RHS.)

In 1851, after years of experimentation, Jesse Williams developed a method to standardize the production of cheese. Using the milk from hundreds of different cows, he was able to produce a uniform-tasting cheese. Although most business in Rome was heavy industry, the dairy farmers contributed greatly to the success of Rome.

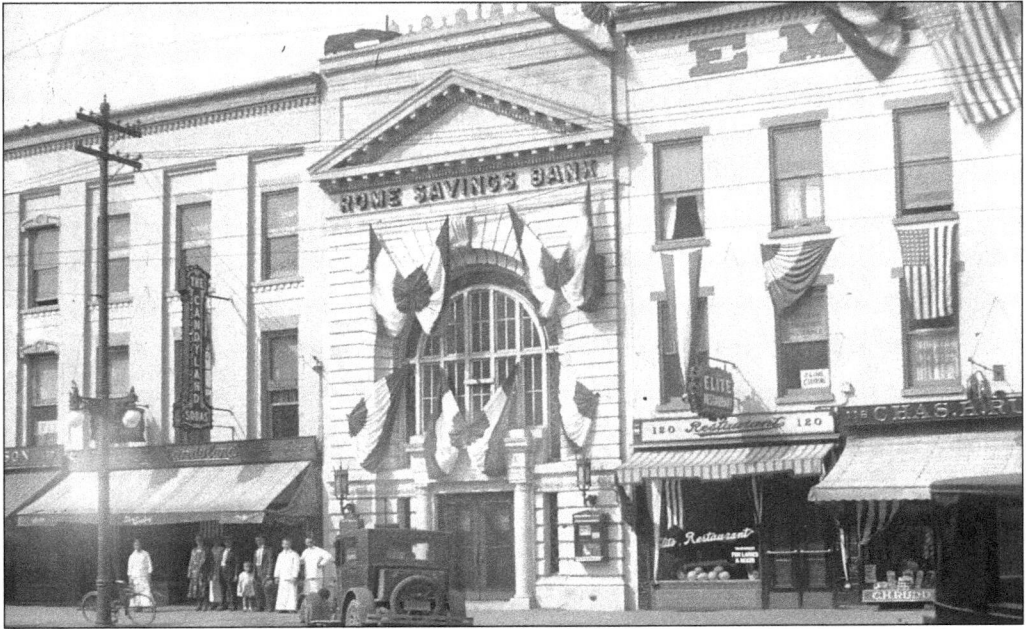

A landmark on Dominick Street is the Rome Savings Bank. Chartered in 1851, this is the oldest bank in Rome still doing business under its original name. This cornerstone of the financial industry continues to grow and prosper, as it now operates four additional branches.

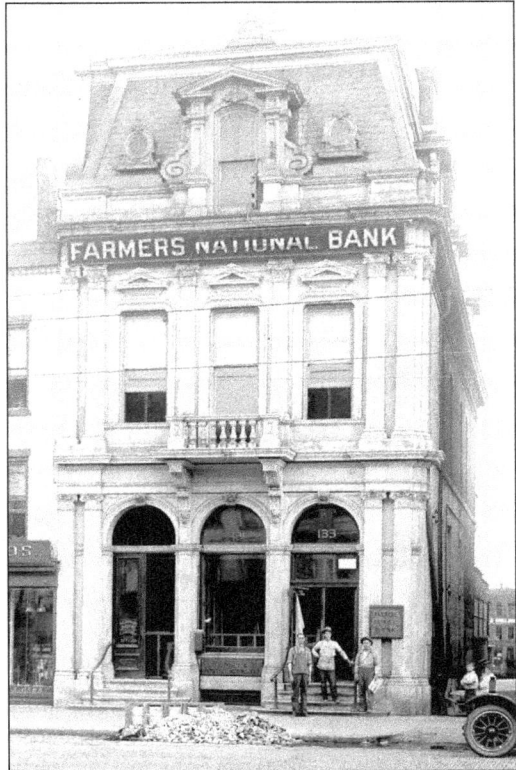

The Second Bank of Rome received its charter in 1875. A reorganization of assets changed the name to the Farmer's National Bank in 1879. It engaged in several forms of domestic and foreign financial transactions and investments. Personal banking services were a preference over industrial accounts.

The Fort Stanwix National Bank opened for business in 1847. It is interesting to note that the Rome Savings Bank, Oneida County Savings Bank, and Fort Stanwix National Bank all shared the same building when it was located on the Saulpaugh Block of South James Street.

In 1915, the biggest financial merger in the history of Rome came when the Rome City Bank and the First National Bank merged to form the Rome Trust Company. The building was a landmark of the American Corner until the urban renewal of the 1960s brought about its destruction.

Three

A STROLL DOWNTOWN

The American Corner, the heart of downtown Rome, was located at the intersections at Dominick and James Streets. Built at the end of the 18th century was a large three-story inn called the American Hotel. The Marquis de La Fayette even spent the night there. Although the hotel was long gone by the turn of the next century, the name had always remained with that intersection.

According to local legend, the outline of Fort Stanwix always appeared as an irregularly shaped star design. Archeological excavations have proven the fort was perfectly geometrical in shape. At the four corners or bastions of the fort, large Civil War–era cannons signified the site of the old fort.

The Rome Club, formerly known as the Barnes-Mudge house, patriotically decorated, stood at 115 Dominick Street. Completed around 1830, this large mansion eventually became home to an elite social club in the 1900s. Also shown is the cannon that marked the west bastion of Fort Stanwix.

The Stryker House located at 112 East Liberty Street was the location of the east bastion of Fort Stanwix. This was another one of Rome's stately mansions of the downtown area constructed around 1839. Named Liberty Hall by the residents, it served as the unofficial headquarters for the Democratic Party in Rome. It was also the first house in Rome to have roof gutters. (RHS.)

This early view shows some Rome Girl Scouts posing on the lawn and cannon of the Stryker House following a Fort Stanwix day celebration in 1922. The south bastion was located at 107 Spring Street, and the north bastion was located at 104 East Liberty Street. (RHS.)

The cornerstone for Rome's first official city hall building on James Street was laid on October 14, 1894. A section of the new administration building was set aside for the Rome Police Department. A new and modern city hall built on Washington Street replaced this structure in the 1970s.

After sharing storefronts with various venues for years, the post office constructed a building devoted solely to that of the mail service in 1903 at the corner of Liberty and James Streets. With the expansion of the mail service, a larger building was constructed at Church Street, and currently it resides on Garden Street.

A disastrous fire in 1847 left Rome without a courthouse and jail. The new courthouse and jail was completed in 1849. Shown above, around the time of the Civil War, are some of Rome's barristers on the front steps. Since the original construction in 1849, several additions have been made over the years.

The Rome Court House is seen as it appeared after a major expansion in 1902. A large dome and vestibule were a few of the many upgrades made. Other than routine maintenance, the courthouse still looks much the same as it did back in 1902.

Presumably the oldest known house in the city of Rome, constructed sometime in the 18th century, was the Empire House. In the house's almost 200 years of existence on Dominick Street, it was a tavern for the frontier settlers. Later the house became the Stanwix Seminary for Young Ladies and a hotel in its later years until its destruction in 1971. (RHS.)

The Temperance Hotel at 210 South James Street was a local institution. Visitors had their choice of 60 well-decorated rooms for $1 a day. One could dine in the spacious dining hall for 25¢. However, one would not find an alcoholic beverage on the premises, hence the name Temperance Hotel.

32

White's Hotel was a very popular resting spot for travelers. It offered a respectable dinning room, a bar, and a reading room. Its location at 226 West Dominick Street was centrally located near the business district and the railway station.

A well-known stop for businessmen traveling through Rome since the 1880s was at the Arlington Hotel. This majestic four-story building occupied the majority of the corner at Washington and Dominick Streets. A portion of the hotel was set aside and used as a hospital at the beginning of the 20th century.

In business since the early part of the 19th century, Stanwix Hall was Rome's oldest and premier hotel known to many famous politicians. Boasting 70 luxurious well-decorated rooms with all the amenities of home is what made Stanwix Hall a favorite among travelers.

Some of the features that made Stanwix Hall stand out from the others and contributed to its popularity among its guests were the large sitting rooms, parlors, reading and writing rooms, a well-stocked bar, a pool and billiard room, and even a barbershop, all located on the lower levels.

The A. M. Jackson Company (right) at 165 West Dominick Street and the F. E. Bacon Company (below) at 185 West Dominick Street both specialized in dry goods. Dry goods were virtually anything from carpets and house furnishings to clothes and apparel. Decorated tastefully in the latest styles, both stores had well-laid-out floor plans. Each of the three stories had wall-to-wall options for the discriminating shopper looking for the necessities of life, or perhaps to splurge on the modern conveniences of life. In the 1930s, the F. E. Bacon Company became Nelson's Department Store, a well-known facet in the downtown district until urban renewal.

F. E. BACON CO.
DRY GOODS, CLOAKS
AND SUITS
ROME, N. Y.

T. W. Perry of 153 West Dominick Street was the home of tailor-made clothing in Rome. It also boasted the largest assortment of men's furnishings in the area. In addition, it had a wide selection of nationally known manufactured clothing brands.

When it came to shoes, the finest selection available was at Thing's Shoe Store at 213 West Dominick Street. It was aggressively advertised as "the Shoe Hustlers" because of its low prices for the whole family. The eye in the sky on the right belongs to that of the neighborhood eye doctor.

"A shave and a hair cut—two bits." The barbers and customers are seen inside the U-R-Next Barber Shop located at 128 North Washington Street inside the Arlington Hotel. On the wall are occupational shaving mugs, each with personalized artwork to a specific regular customer's occupation.

Another common sight in old Rome was the many peddlers walking up and down the streets, hawking their wares to wanting customers. One could find everything for sale, from fruits and vegetables, to freshly slaughtered meats, to household goods. The peddler was as important to the business success of the city as any brick-and-mortar store.

A trip to the corner "chemist" would always be a welcome relief from any ailment of the day. In the early 1900s, medicines did not come conveniently prepackaged; they were made to order by the chemist. Vulgar by today's standards, note the spittoon in the aisle.

While waiting for the chemist to prepare their orders for medication, customers could peruse the large selection of domestic and imported cigars, soda, and candy offered for sale at the United Chemists–United Cigar shop at the American Corner.

In the middle of Upstate New York, there are many opportunities to fish and hunt. To satisfy the needs of sportsmen, Cahill's at 113 North James Street was there to deliver. A successful hunt is displayed outside the store. The black bear is not something one sees too often in Rome. (RHS.)

The new recreational sport sensation following World War I was the motorcycle. A gang of Romans poses in front of Albert Noonan's store at 105 East Dominick Street. The signage indicates that Noonan specialized in the sale of Indian motorcycles. (RHS.)

The white truck of the White Laundry service makes its rounds throughout Rome for its store located at 140 North Washington Street. "Put your duds into our suds" was its famous motto known very well by the clientele.

From the farm to the home was the only way one could receive fresh milk in the days before modern refrigeration. It was not an item available at the corner store. A deliveryman from the Marshall Dairy is making a daily delivery to a residence.

Every city needed a corner ice-cream parlor. Charles Milvo was there to feed the needs of Romans for many years from his 141 North James Street store. In addition to his delicious homemade ice cream, he offered a wide selection of fresh fruits for sale.

Next to Milvo's store was the office of the Rome Gas and Electric Power Company. The year 1852 saw the installation of the first gas lamps in Rome. Electricity soon followed around 1885, ending the need for lamplighters. A repair truck is on the scene doing work near the Kingsley Block on North James Street.

At the main tracks of the New York Central Railroad located on South James Street near the Ethridge Block, one could find accommodations at the Powers House. Rooms for $1 a day and 25¢ meals tempted visitors near the depot. According to the sign at the left, it has ladies dining rooms.

Bartenders await the rush in one of the many drinking establishments that catered to the need of the thirsty mill worker when his shift was over. Rome was also home to a handful of breweries, the largest being Evans and Giehl that produced Rome Ale. Another familiar brew was Fort Stanwix Ale.

MARCH 17 1906 A.C. KESSINGER (No.1) PRESIDENT OF THE ROME SENTINEL COMPANY, ROME N.Y. STARTED TO LEARN THE PRINTER'S TRADE AT THE AGE OF 14. THIS PHOTO WAS TAKEN IN THE ROME DAILY SENTINEL PRESS ROOM, MARCH 17. 1922. BY C.B. HOWLAND.

Romans still depend on the *Rome Daily Sentinel* as their only daily source of printed news, as they have since 1851. The first edition of the *Sentinel* went into print in 1821 as a weekly edition, and it did not become a daily newspaper until 1851. Originally located on James Street near the post office, it is now located on Dominick Street.

Jervis Library, Rome. N.Y.

John Bloomfield Jervis spent his youth as an engineer on the Erie Canal project and later on many railroad projects earning national acclaim. Ten years following his death in 1895, per his request, Jervis donated his 1857 homestead to be a public library. The library continually serves the needs of Romans after several additions to the original building were completed.

Dominick Street, in this view looking west around 1960, had changed little over the years. The urban renewal projects of the 1970s would remove this road and the majority of the buildings shown and replace them with a modern city hall, parking garages, and a pedestrian mall. Photographs are all that remain of the once mighty downtown.

James Street seen south around 1960 from the old city hall area also changed very little over the years. Demolition of every building shown above made way for the National Park Service's recreation of Fort Stanwix and the Tomb of the Unknown Revolutionary War Soldier.

Four

RELIGION AND EDUCATION

As the small community grew into a thriving metropolis, so did the need for religious worship. Shown above is the interior of St. John the Baptist Roman Catholic Church on River Street. The large Italian population in the surrounding area represented this small church. In 1954, it relocated to the corner of Dominick and River Streets, where it still stands today, serving a new generation of Italian Americans.

St. Peter's Roman Catholic Church is the oldest Catholic organization in Rome. Under the tenure of Rev. William Beecham, the first St. Peter's was built around 1840 on the site of the old state arsenal along the Mohawk River. Rev. Aloysius Murphy oversaw the construction of the present-day St. Peter's, which was completed in 1897 on James Street. It was one of the few buildings not razed for the reconstruction of Fort Stanwix. At the top of River Street, St. Aloysius Academy Catholic School was a renovation of the old church. In the same area, the Sisters of the Holy Name opened a boarding school for women.

The early settlers of Rome drafted a compact to form a religious society. The result of that initial meeting was the First Presbyterian Church. Its first formal meetinghouse was built in 1808 in the town square. The present-day church opened in 1852. A magnificent copper-covered steeple rises 180 feet into the air.

The congregation of the Cavalry Methodist Episcopal Church poses in front of its Madison Street meetinghouse under the leadership of Rev. Charles Miller. The Methodist movement started in Rome in the late 18th century.

Jonathan Newman started the First Methodist Episcopal group during 1799 in Rome. The group dedicated its first church in 1829 on East Court Street, and it was the first in America to have a steeple. It moved to a larger structure on North George Street in 1869. Even with several additions, the church remains an active part of the religious community today.

August 15, 1825, brought the Zionist movement to Rome. In 1851, Richard Upjohn, a famous architect, designed a Gothic-inspired church for the parishioners. This architectural marvel houses lavish stained-glass windows crafted by the Tiffany Art Glass Studios of New York. It resides at the corner of Liberty and Washington Streets.

The First Baptist Church is the most historically important in Rome. The first meetings took place in 1817. Churches were built in 1826 and the present-day church at the corner of George and Embargo Streets. Rev. David Bellamy's son, Francis Bellamy, penned the "Pledge of Allegiance" in 1892. His original 23-word poem sparked a wave of patriotism throughout the country. How fitting an honor for a city already steeped in the early history of the American flag.

Baptist Church, Rome, N.Y.

To serve the Catholic German parishioners of the factory village area of Rome was St. Mary's Church on Liberty Street. Complementing the church built in 1872 is an impressive tower containing three bells and a magnificent steeple. Located next to the church was an elementary school and rectory.

The history of the early educational system of Rome is rather vague other than several small one-room and private schools serving the needs of the village. In 1840, a private boarding school opened known as the Rome Academy, and in 1869, it became a "free" school. From that point on, education in the city was free to the students. The first graduating class of Rome Free Academy consisted of four students.

By the early 1900s, the old Rome Free Academy had become obsolete in every way and had to be demolished. A new school with a French-inspired design took its place in 1899. In 1926, the school was converted into a junior high school and was used until its demolition in 1959. The police station now stands there at the corner of James and Court Streets.

The third Rome Free Academy built on Turin Road opened its doors for the 1926 school year. A disastrous fire in 1938 almost destroyed the school. It was necessary to transfer classes to the other schools while repairs were completed. Several expansions between 1958 and 1963 included a new football stadium. The school remained in use until the current Rome Free Academy opened at the Griffiss Technology Park in 2001.

The brick school on Liberty Street specialized in elementary education. A nicely designed art deco building constructed in 1910 replaced the aging original 1870s structure. This school was renamed Barringer in honor of longtime principal Roemer Barringer. The American Red Cross is currently using the building.

No.1 - Miss Lena M. Putnam, Principal
Jay St. Graduating Class. Photo by C.B.Hov. June 1919.

The Jay Street School was another of Rome's early educational buildings dating back to the 1870s. The building still stands today much the same as it did back in 1876 at its location at 500 North Jay Street, except it is now an apartment building.

Another relic of the early school system was the East Rome School on Third Street, built in 1874 and enlarged in 1915. To honor the longtime principal Lillian O. Burns, the school's name was changed. The building is now an apartment building.

The Rome City School District saw its largest expansion at the beginning of the 20th century when several new schools were constructed. The Thomas Street School was one of them and opened in 1912. The name changed to Harvey Alter some years later. Today it serves as the headquarters for the board of education and the office of the superintendent.

Gansevoort Elementary School opened in 1914 at 758 West Liberty Street. It is interesting to note that while studying the edifice of the building one can see that there are separate entrances for boys and girls. Most classes of the day were also segregated by gender.

The building at 110 West Linden Street is home to Fort Stanwix School, constructed in 1920. Today the school specializes in elementary education. Education in the early 20th century focused on domestic skills for the ladies to prepare them for the family life. Many students never graduated, as they were needed to help support their families. Below, the students of Mrs. Henry Barnard's class are learning how to make sugar cookies.

PHOTO BY C.B. HOWLAND,
FORT STANWIX SCHOOL, 8-A CLASS, MAKING SUGAR COOKIES, MAY 21 1925, ROME, N.Y.
MRS. HENRY BARNARD (No.1) DOMESTIC SCIENCE INSTRUCTOR

While the ladies were honing their domestic skills, the young men were learning the finer techniques of wood- and metalworking. Since Rome was a highly industrialized city, these skills were always in demand by local industry. It was not uncommon for 16-year-olds to drop out of school to take a factory job to help support their families. Many worked at the same factory for 40 or 50 years.

The Willett Street School was on the corner of James and Ridge Streets. It was a specialized trade school for many years. In 1959, the parishioners of Transfiguration Church purchased it from the school district and converted it to a Catholic school. Volunteers completely refurbished the building from top to bottom. Waning enrollment in Catholic schools forced the school to close, and it fell to the wrecker's ball.

The West Rome School provided educational opportunities to the students who lived in the outer districts. It was the most simply designed of all the new schools. Later it helped only students with special needs, especially those who were severely mentally handicapped.

The premier institution for the hearing impaired is the Central New York Institution for Deaf Mutes, now known as the New York State School for the Deaf, located on a massive campus at 711–733 North Madison Street. The school became a reality through the generosity of several wealthy Romans in 1875. A new, modern campus has since replaced the old buildings. The quality of the education remains unsurpassed in the state.

Catholic education began in Rome in 1865 when the Sisters of the Holy Names of Jesus and Mary began to teach the children of St. Peter's and St. Mary's parishes. Located at the crest of River Street, St. Peter's Academy evolved into the Academy of the Holy Names, which became a private young ladies' boarding school. The majestic grounds had wooded paths, lavish gardens, and even a small private lake justly named Sister's Pond. The academic buildings had lavish decorations in a classic motif and boasted a grand music room complete with a harp. This remarkable institution closed in 1963.

Showing Boat House Academy of Holy Names. Rome N.Y.

St. Aloysius Academy began classes in 1897 in the renovated original St. Peter's Church on top of River Street. Little was left of the original 1838 facade after the renovations. Baseball games for St. A's were always a favorite pastime for many Romans. The building was torn down in 1963, and St. Peter's elementary school opened in its place.

MAY, 14, 1926. No. 1
THE NEW ST. MARY'S SCHOOL, ROME, N.Y. FATHER HEISLER, PASTOR.
FATHER HEMMER, ASSISTANT PASTOR. PHOTO BY C.B. HOWLAND, ROME.

Rome has the privilege to have a well-rounded education system including parochial schools. St. Mary's School originally catered to the needs of the German immigrants. The Franciscan Sisterhood comprised most of the staff at their school located on Liberty Street.

Five

TO SERVE AND PROTECT

As soon as the village of Rome incorporated in 1819, the need for a fire department was an early concern. Volunteer organizations complete with a horse and hand pump formed Rome's first fire department. In addition to the hand pump, many early homes kept buckets ready in the event of a fire. The citizens would then form a bucket brigade, passing the buckets from the water source to the fire manually. Fires were extremely disastrous, and it was not at all uncommon to lose an entire city block to fire. The two volunteer Rome firemen above were photographed sometime in 1854. The fireman on the right is also holding a speaking trumpet, which was used to amplify his voice at the scene of a fire.

This Civil War–era photograph is of the Fort Stanwix Engine No. 2 and the Mohawk Hose Company No. 2 at the East Liberty Street Fire Station. Shown is the first steam-powered fire engine used by the Rome Fire Department. Several expansions were made to this station that would eventually be the headquarters of the fire department.

A member of the Washington Hose Company No. 3 proudly poses in his elaborate dress uniform. Rome had hundreds of volunteers until the city established a paid fire department in 1891. Some of the volunteer companies were named: Gansevoort Engine No. 1, Independence Hose No. 1, Rome Hook and Ladder No. 1, Stryker Hose No. 1, Fort Stanwix Hose No. 2, Mohawk Hose No. 2, and Washington Hose No. 3.

With the formation of the Rome Fire Department as a professional paid department, a chief and eight engineers were hired to protect the city. The paid department still relied on the help of the volunteer companies into the 1950s. The department utilized three fire stations. Station House No. 1 located at 216 North Washington Street remained operational through 1965.

Station House No. 3 served the canal district on South George Street. It remained in use through 1920, when it closed and the equipment transferred to Station No. 2. The building today is a private residence. (RHS.)

Station House No. 2 was the largest of the Rome fire stations and served as the headquarters. All of the alarm boxes in the city fed into the Gamewell Alarm System, as seen in the picture below. From here, an alarm would sound and the men would rush into action. Harnesses would drop onto the horses, a fireman would stoke the steam engine, the doors would burst open, and the horses would charge down the streets with bells a blazing to the scene of the fire. This was the glamour of the "romantic era" of firefighting.

The horse-drawn hose truck No. 1 takes a moment to pose for the camera. Horses were a vital part of the firefighting effort and as such were very well taken care of. Some of the names of the horses included Mose, Tige, Babe, Dick, Fred, and Billy, although, Billy was actually a police horse that was transferred to the fire department.

One of the city's two fire engines belches steam as it provides the necessary relay of water from the hydrant to the fireman's nozzle. Following the fatal Elm Row fire in 1866, when fireman Phillip Bickel was killed in the blaze, the first steamer was purchased. He is the only Rome firefighter to have died in a fire. (RHS.)

Firemen practice on the spring-loaded Hayes aerial truck ladder near the Liberty Street fire station. Fire Chief Leonard Briggs is posing in the center. The Hayes ladder was necessary for rescues considering a majority of the buildings in Rome were more than one story, especially the factories. The photograph below shows a side view, and in it a folded life net can be seen. The technology was very simplistic; a group of firemen and bystanders would hold the net, and the victim would jump away from the burning building into the net. Scary, but it worked.

The Rome Fire Department also relied on volunteers until the 1950s to assist with firefighting duties. Also assisting the paid department were volunteer brigades located inside the factories. In the above photograph are members of the Romeoid Hose Company at the Rome Wire Company.

The automobile eventually sealed the fate of the horse-drawn fire equipment. Rome purchased its first motorized apparatus in 1915, an American LaFrance triple combination engine. By 1925, the fire department was fully motorized.

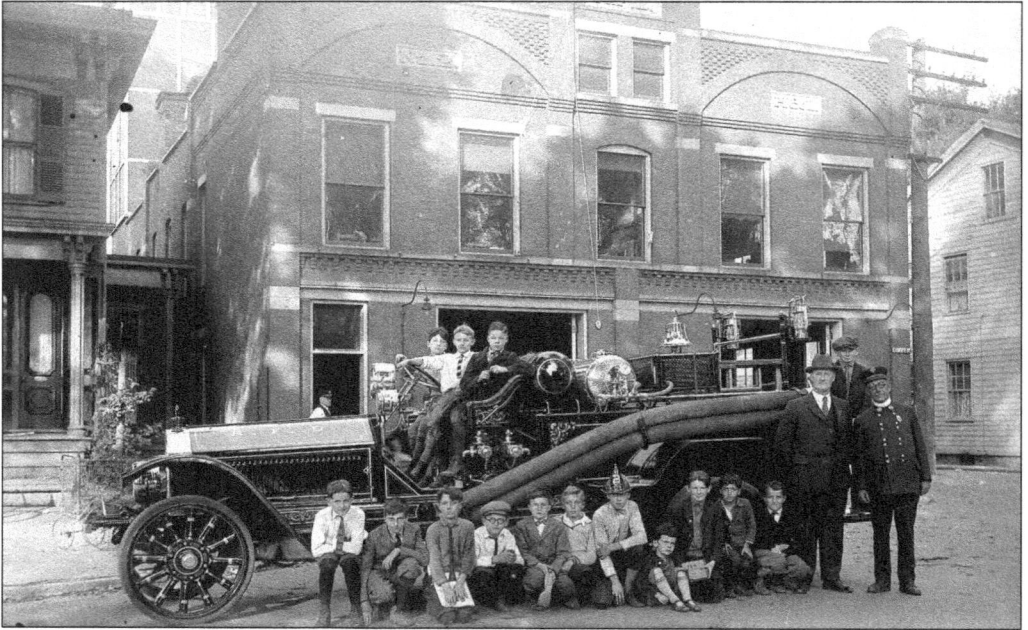

Every kid's dream to become a firefighter is being lived by this group of children. The chief along with his junior department are proudly posing in front of the newly purchased Ward LaFrance engine.

Disasters came in many different forms. Fire was the biggest enemy of buildings, but many natural disasters like floods and blizzards required the intervention of the fire department. Train derailments were another hazard, as well as industrial accidents.

A small fire quickly spreads into a catastrophic firestorm fueled by old dry timbers and the close proximity of the adjoining building. A whole city block was completely engulfed in flames, and the firemen could do little to stop it. It is interesting to note that the majority of Rome's most disastrous fires took place in the winter.

All that remains of Sink's Opera House located at 104–108 East Dominick Street is shown here. The June 28, 1904, fire left an icon of the entertainment world in ruins. Well known throughout Upstate New York, Sink's Opera House had many famous actors and actresses perform on its stage.

One of the more devastating fires in Rome occurred on February 2, 1908. A fire broke out in the F. E. Bacon store on West Dominick Street and quickly spread to the adjoining buildings. Before long the Ethridge, Benner, and Hammond Blocks were all ablaze. The Rome Fire Department and scores of volunteers battled the blaze throughout the freezing cold day, eventually extinguishing the fire. Although a large portion of Dominick Street lay in ruins, it was quickly rebuilt.

The average snowfall in Rome tops 100 inches a year. Combined with the unpredictable spring weather of thawing and then refreezing, ice dams would form. This would cause the Mohawk River to back up and begin flooding into lowlands near the banks. The bridge shown above the Mohawk River is at flood stage.

Among the residential areas around the Mohawk River, River Street certainly lived up to its name. A springtime flood appears in the photograph above. The construction of the dam at Lake Delta in 1912 helped to regulate the flow of the Mohawk more efficiently, and major flooding stopped.

The fall of 1945 was a wet one. On October 1, a tremendous amount of rain fell and caused the water to flow off the dam at Lake Delta. Unable to control the flow of water, the Mohawk River flooded for the first time since the dam was finished in 1912. As the water flowed down the raging Mohawk River, many locations began to flood. The water rose so fast in the River Street area that the floodwaters were almost four feet high within a short period. The fire and police departments had to rescue and evacuate people by boat. The flood spread to East Dominick Street and as far away as First Street. After two days, the floodwaters receded and life was back to normal in Rome.

Four juvenile delinquents on the morning of November 19, 1895, used stolen tools to dislodge several rails on the New York Central Railroad tracks in an attempt to derail a mail train that they were going to rob. The train derailed, and all the cars fell off the track except for the passenger car. The engineer and two hitchhikers died in the crash, and 11 passengers were injured. All four hoodlums were sentenced to life in prison. Two subsequently died in prison, and the governor pardoned the other two in 1906.

Hundreds of trains passed through Rome on a weekly basis, and travel was relatively safe. Every now and then, a train derailment would occur, like this one in 1910. The wreck happened just outside Rome on the New York Central Railroad line. Only the engineer suffered minor injuries in this wreck.

Ferlo's store located on South James Street was a favorite stop for engines on the New York Central Railroad line. The above photograph shows a derailment that happened on November 4, 1906. The engineer and the brakeman died in the wreck. The wreck shown in the photograph below took place on July 7, 1908, also crashing into Ferlo's. Only minor injuries were the result of that wreck. Note the circuslike atmosphere of the crowds assembled in both of the photographs. (RHS.)

Armed with clubs, pride, and the law, Rome's very own "Keystone Coppers" are on patrol downtown near the American Corner in the early 1900s.

The Rome Police Department and mascot of 1907 were photographed in front of their headquarters at city hall. Until the 1880s, Rome only had a chief, a constable, and a handful of night watchmen to police the city. Since this 1907 photograph, the police department has increased tenfold. (RHS.)

PHILIP S. McDONALD
1867 - 1920

On December 15, 1920, officer Phillip McDonald found himself in the middle of an armed robbery. The robbery led to a car chase, and McDonald followed the suspects all the way to Herkimer and was killed by an automobile. He remains Rome's only police officer to make the supreme sacrifice in the line of duty. In the photograph below, his fellow officers carry McDonald's remains out of St. Peter's Church. McDonald was a 19-year veteran of the department.

Shown in the composite photograph of the Rome Police Department are some uniformed and plainclothes officers who made up the department in 1928. In 1915, the Rome Police Department began to motorize the force. At first there was the motorcycle officer, three years later a Cadillac patrol car and ambulance went into service. Several more cars and motorcycles steadily joined the ranks over the next decade. Originally the police force ran the ambulance service. However, that is a function since absorbed by the fire department and private companies. The current police building stands on the site occupied by the old high school on the corner of James and Court Streets. (RHS.)

City Hospital, Rome, N.Y.

No citywide institution for health care existed in Rome before 1940. The Rome Hospital located on East Garden Street was the largest of all the small private hospitals that served the needs of the sick. Others included the Arlington Hotel, the Rose Hospital, and the Murphy Memorial Hospital.

Located at 506 West Embargo Street on Thorn's Pond, Murphy Memorial Hospital utilized the old homestead for its infirmary. In the 1930s, it converted its services solely to maternity care. The Kennedy Skating Arena now stands over this site.

Conditions deteriorated at all of the small hospitals throughout the city. In 1940, the Rome Hospital and the Murphy Memorial Hospital pooled their resources together and opened a large hospital on North James Street and called it the Rome Murphy Memorial Hospital, which remains Rome's only hospital.

Dr. Willey J. P. Kingsley and his sons ran one of the unique medical facilities in Rome. They opened their sanitarium at 120 East Park Street in 1859. Dr. Kingsley pioneered the treatment for various cancers of the body, and he claimed to have cured tens of thousands of people of this ailment in his lifetime. Dr. Kingsley was also an important part of the economic growth of Rome, and he served two terms as mayor from 1895 to 1899.

The Oneida County Home was located on upper Floyd Avenue near the Mohawk River. Originally a poorhouse, the county home took in those considered wards of the county. In addition, many patients suffered from physical and mental handicaps. The Oneida County Home consisted of several outbuildings, a hospital, and farmlands. It boarded well over 300 people at a time.

The State Custodial Asylum, later the Rome State School, was an expanded version of the Oneida County Home. Located outside the city on lower James Street, the asylum consisted of many dormitories for men, women, and children. The research and progress made at the Rome State School over the years on patients suffering from severe physical and mental handicaps has been priceless. As more and more of the patients integrated back into the local community, the state converted the grounds into a prison called the Oneida Correctional Facility at Rome.

Six

THE WORLD AT WAR

The federal government purchased a parcel of land from Dominick Lynch in 1814 to construct an arsenal. Heavy supplies and ordnance were specialties of the federal arsenal at Rome located on Dominick Street near Wood Creek. In the 70-year existence of the arsenal, there were 10 different commanders. All that remains today is the commander's house as shown. This picture was taken in the 1870s; note the guards on the front porch.

(Those Marked thus (*) are Alive)

1 Gen. Rufus Daggett	7 Surgeon H. W. Carpenter	13 Capt. Edward Downer	19 Lieut. Wm. Appleton
2 Col. Wm. R. Pease	8 Capt. J. F. Kerrigan	14 Capt. Harrison Pease	20 Adj. Chas. S. Millard
3 Lieut.-Col. F. X. Myers	9 Capt. Jas. M. Lattimore	15 Capt. Geo. W. Brigham	21 Lieut. Alonzo Denison
4 Lieut.-Col. Egbert Bagg	10 Capt. Edward Warr	16 Capt. John H. Fairbanks	22 Lieut. Geo. W. Ross
5 Brevet-Maj. Wm. L. Bartholomew	11 Capt. Frank H. Lay	17 Capt. Wm. L. Hurlbut	23 Lieut. Morris Chappell
6 Brevet-Maj. D. B. Magill	12 Capt. L. K. Brown	18 Lieut. Spencer C. Meyer	24 Lieut. John G. Glazier

A call for new volunteers went out in the summer of 1862. Col. William Pease, a West Point graduate, was to lead the new regiment of 1,000 men. The state's official designation was the 117th New York State Volunteers. Many volunteers continued to flock into the recruiting stations and Col. Kenner Garrard, another West Pointer, formed another regiment, the 146th New York State Volunteers in Rome. Both regiments trained in Rome at Camp Huntington located around Expense Street.

In 1863, the 146th New York adopted the Zouave style of uniform, as worn by the drum corps shown above. The 146th participated in all of the major battles of the Army of the Potomac from Gettysburg to the surrender of Confederates at Appomatox Court House. It lost half its strength at the Battle of the Wilderness alone and was one of the hardest-fighting regiments in the war.

A successful crockery merchant named Charles Skillin led Rome's militia called the Gansevoort Guards. At the outbreak of the Civil War, Skillin and several members of the militia mustered into the 14th New York State Volunteers in 1861. Skillin received a commission to the rank of lieutenant colonel and became the first Roman to die in the war, leading a charge at the Battle of Gaines Mills in Virginia.

Skillin Post No. 47 Grand Army of the Republic was named in honor of Lt. Col. Charles Skillin. In a store window is a memorial photograph of Gen. Ulysess S. Grant, which would date this photograph to 1885. Bradford Tompkins, one of Rome's African American soldiers, is also pictured in the back. (RHS.)

All that remains of the mighty warriors of the 146th New York is pictured on the steps of the courthouse at a 1920 reunion. Their bravery is clearly distinguished on a battle flag in the background and the relics that surround them.

Time became the biggest enemy for the Civil War veteran. The number of surviving veterans dwindled each year, and when this photograph was taken in 1922, there were roughly 30. There were five remaining in 1935, and the last surviving member of the war, Joseph Chisam, passed in 1947, ending this era of Rome's history. (RHS.)

Members of the Fort Stanwix Guard take a moment out of drilling to pose for this 1875 picture. Several small militias existed in Rome in the years leading up to World War I. Seen in the background off to the right is the original 1838 St. Peter's Church located at the top of River Street.

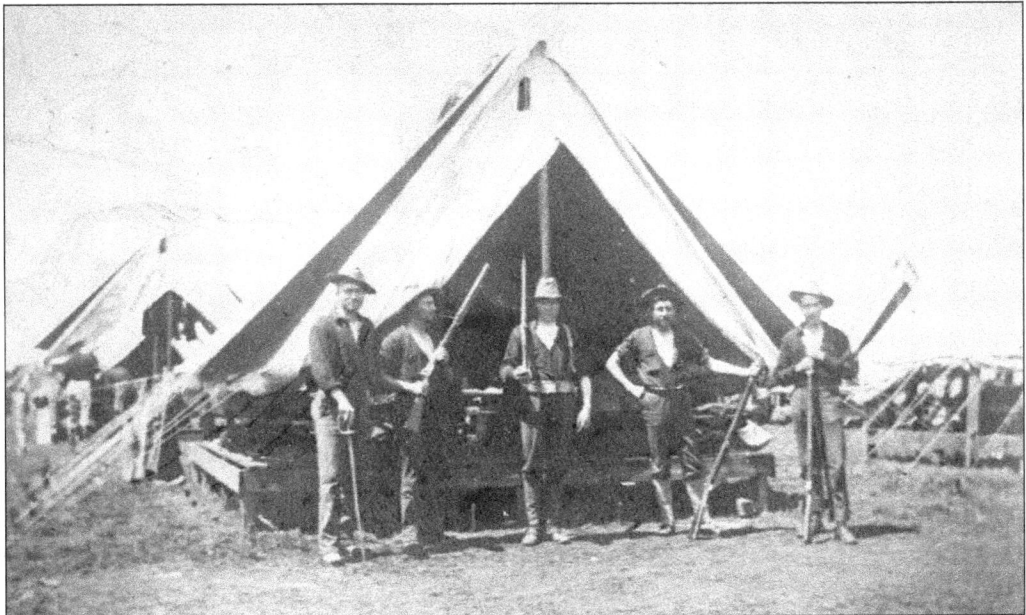

Several Romans found their way into Company K of the 202nd New York Volunteers in the Spanish-American War of 1898. The 202nd was the first regiment to march through the streets of Havana, Cuba. They remained at Camp Barrett for several months to help restore their shattered infrastructure. Pvt. Frederick Schroth, at left, was Rome's last surviving Spanish-American War veteran.

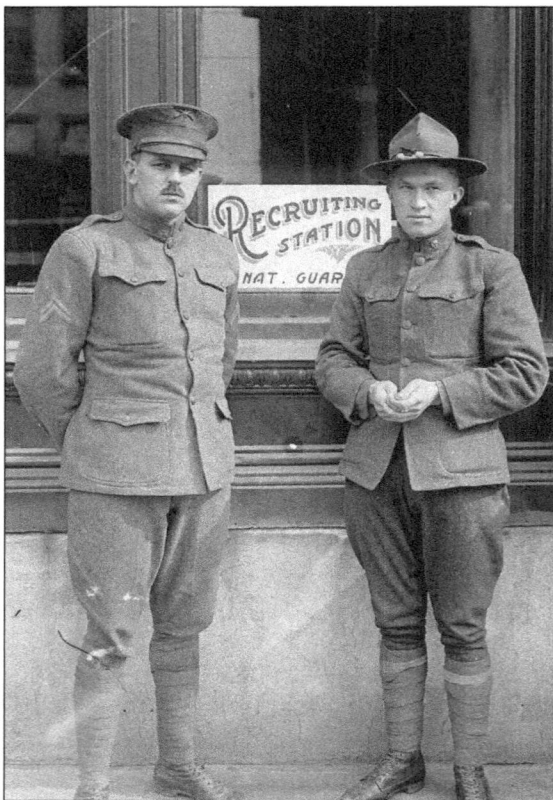

When the United States entered World War I, recruiting stations opened throughout the state to fill federally mandated enlistment quotas. Rome's quota was 246 men. Two of Rome's recruiters are shown eagerly awaiting volunteers to enlist. In all, 1,398 men and 15 women enlisted to serve in the armed forces from Rome.

The 23rd Machine Gun Company formed and remained behind in Rome as the "home guard" unit. It fell under the command of the National Guard with the purpose of defending the state if needed.

With war comes a heavy toll. On July 8, 1918, Cpl. Henry P. Smith was killed in action and was the first Roman to fall in that conflict. An honor guard and caisson carry the flag-draped remains of Smith to the cemetery. The local Veterans of Foreign Wars post bears his name.

When the war ended on November 18, 1918, 40 Romans had made the ultimate sacrifice for their country. The city commissioned a special medal for the veterans, and a citywide welcome home celebration took place on October 4, 1919. Many Romans back from the war marched down James Street to a heroes' welcome.

Veterans of the 27th Infantry Division pose in front of the courthouse at the welcome home ceremonies. The 27th was made up primarily of New York recruits who had seen some of the fiercest battles of the war.

Veteran sailors are pictured at the welcome home ceremonies in 1919. One cannot overlook the importance of the navy in the great conflict. The navy was the essential lifeline needed to bring in troops and supplies to the armies in the field. (RHS.)

Romans of the U.S. Marine Corps stand at ease during the welcome home ceremonies. One of the marines is holding a comical sign, and note the wide variety of uniforms they are sporting in the picture.

The 10th Medical Detachment of the New York National Guard was organized at Rome in 1926. The army federalized the 10th Medical Detachment into service shortly after the bombing of Pearl Harbor in 1941. Its destination was the pacific theater, where it served with distinction.

No words could ever describe the bravery and sacrifice made by thousands of Romans that served in the armed forces and on the home front. The City of Rome bestowed a medal upon the veterans of World War II, and the certificate above sums up the sentiments of many Romans.

The War Department announced in the summer of 1941 that Rome would become home to an air depot. Construction, overseen by Turner-Mayersohn, began in the fall of 1941. After the attack on Pearl Harbor, construction of the depot was a top priority for the War Department. Runways, buildings, and hangars rose in record time, with the Rome Air Depot opening for service in February 1942.

The supply depot building has seen many missions, and it is one of the last original buildings from the Rome Air Depot still used by the government. Today the building houses the Defense Finance and Accounting Service, which is one of the largest employers in Rome.

The combined mission of the depot was maintenance and repair of airplanes. The B-29 above needed some engine repairs before it returned to the war zone. The B-29 became the icon of air superiority for the United States after the *Enola Gay* dropped the first atomic bombs on Japan, ending World War II.

With the advent of the cold war, the U.S. Air Force (USAF) took control of the depot in 1947 and renamed the base Griffiss. It was named in honor of Lt. Col. Townsend Griffiss, the first aviator killed in World War II. The original triangle-shaped runways are seen alongside the two-and-a-quarter-mile runway built in the 1950s. Rome's geographic location again made it home to another formidable fortress. (USAF.)

First came the fighter planes of the 27th and 465th Fighter Interceptor Squadrons (FIS) charged with protecting the Northeast Air Defense Sector. Armed with the F-106 Dart, the 49th FIS took over that mission in 1959. In the picture, its famed falcon tail markings are seen. When the unit deactivated in 1987, it boasted some of the most highly trained fighter pilots in the USAF. (USAF.)

The next flying mission to arrive in 1959 was air refueling. Several KC-135 Stratotankers were assigned to the 41st Air Refueling Squadron (AREFS) at Griffiss. The first tanker that landed took on the name of *The City of Rome*. The 41st AREFS remained at Griffiss until its deactivation in 1995. (USAF.)

Airman 2nd Class Peter Leonard guards a KC-135 of the 41st AREFS during the Cuban Missile Crisis in 1962. This photograph titled "SAC (Strategic Air Command) Sentry Stands Guard" went on to win the Best Photo of the 8th Air Force and then took the honor of being the Best SAC Photo in 1963. (USAF.)

The last flying mission to land at Griffiss was the B-52 Stratofortress in 1960. At first they were assigned to the 4039th Strategic Wing, which was later redesignated the 416th Bombardment Wing in 1963. In 1970, Strategic Air Command took over operations at the base. In 1982, the 416th received the first operational nuclear air-launched cruise missiles. B-52s and KC-135s from Griffiss supported bombing operations during the Vietnam War and Operation Desert Storm. The Base Realignment and Closure Committee ordered that all flying and military support missions at Griffiss would cease operations in 1995, and all units deactivated. With the closure came a loss of over 5,000 jobs. The only military missions that remain are the Air Force Research Laboratory (formerly Rome Lab), DFAS, and the Northeast Air Defense Sector operations. (USAF.)

Seven

SPORTS AND RECREATION

Football has always been a favorite sport in Rome. Hundreds of people still turn out on Friday night to see the Rome Free Academy's Black Knights in action. The above picture shows the 1892 school year football team. The scantiness of the uniforms did not provide much protection, and thankfully there were no serious injuries.

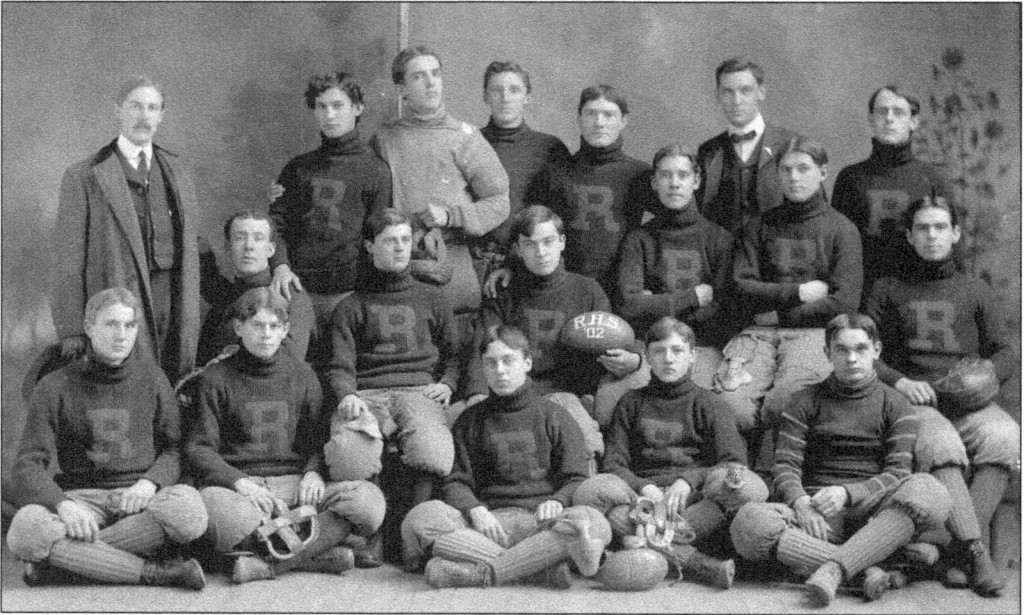

This is the 1902 Black Knights team photograph. A Rome tradition after playing and beating their long-time rivals, Utica Free Academy, the Black Nights, along with the fans, would carry a coffin to the Mohawk River and throw it in. The coffin would float to Utica, symbolizing the killing UFA just experienced.

Baseball was a very popular sport in Rome. It is not known when the first game was played in Rome, but it was well established by the early 1900s. Shown is an undated Rome Free Academy team photograph. Judging by the jester style of their uniforms, it appears it is the late 19th century.

94

Many Romans played the game of baseball, and there were many different teams. Most of the major factories had teams that played in semiprofessional leagues, the most popular being the Empire League. Shown in both of the photographs is pennant day at Riverside Park in 1920. The Rome Wire Company team went on to defeat Diamond Branch that day. In the background, the actual pennant can be seen. Shown below are all the players who participated that day.

The Rome Colonels were as close to professional baseball as could be found in Rome. They were members of the Canadian-American League (Can-Am). The team played its first game in 1937. Its field was located at the present site of the armory off Black River Boulevard. Although the team was a popular local attraction, it was not financially productive and its last season was in 1952.

Listening to the 1920 World Series via radio broadcasting outside the Sentinel's office was a crowd of delighted fans. The Cleveland Indians went on to beat the Brooklyn Dodgers in a nine-game series. It was also the first World Series in which a grand slam home run was hit.

The Church League was another well-liked source of baseball entertainment in Rome. Shown on the steps of its school is the 1923 St. Aloysius Academy baseball team.

Posing for the camera is the 1903 Rome Free Academy women's basketball team. Basketball was another popular team sport of the era, enjoyed by many. Several leagues and teams formed, with the majority of the games played at the YMCA. It was at a YMCA in Massachusetts that the game was first played in 1892. It was through the efforts of the YMCAs in America that the game grew in popularity.

Boxing is one way of solving disputes. Two fighters shake hands before their match at the Oneida County Fair in Rome. A large crowd of men have gathered around to see these men battle in the squared circle.

Renowned for its swimming pool and Saturday morning gatherings was the Rome Women's Club at 110 East Liberty Street. The local Girl Scouts set up their headquarters here as well. Shown in the picture are Girl Scouts who also happen to be American Red Cross lifeguards for the swimming pool.

WORLD'S RECORD HELD BY BRYANT, 1912, FOR SINGLE AMERICAN, BROKEN BY, DR. PAUL W. CROUCH OF BOSTON MASS, NATIONAL ARCHERY CHAMPION, WON AT ROME, N.Y. AUG. 18, 19, 20, 21, 1925. PHOTO BY C.B. HOWLAND, PHOTO. No. 3. ROME, AUG. 20, 1925.

Archery is a sport that requires skill, good aim, and a steady hand. Rome hosted several tournaments like the ones pictured in these photographs in 1925. In the photograph below, the main building of the Rome School for the Deaf can be seen in the background. At this tournament hosted by the National Archery Association, Dr. Paul Crouch broke the world's record, previously set in 1912. Dorothy Smith took high honors in the women's competition.

ANNUAL TOURNAMENT OF THE NATIONAL ARCHERY ASSOCIATION, HELD AT, ROME, N.Y. AUG. 18, 19, 20, 21, 1925. PHOTO BY C.B. HOWLAND, ROME. No. 1

99

Roller-skating was another favorite pastime of Romans. The Palace Roller Rink located at East Court Street had two floors open for customers to use. An elaborate music machine was on the ground level, and there was a stage for live music for the skaters upstairs.

The Rome Country Club in Stanwix and Teugega Country Club located on the shore of Lake Delta provided a welcome rest stop following a challenging round of 18 holes of golf.

FRANK J. MARSHALL, U.S. CHESS CHAMPION, JUST AFTER DEFEATING SEVENTEEN ROMANS AT THE GAME. Y.M.C.A. FLASHLIGHT BY C.B. HOWLAND, ROME, N.Y. APRIL. 8. 1922.

PRESS REP.
R.G.S. HOWLAND

A. HOLLIS.

L.S. SPEAR.

C. SEARLE.

HON. W.E. SCRIPTURE – D.F. SEARLE.

E.L. O'DONNELL.

F.J. MARSHALL.

J. HOOPER.

P. SCRIPTURE.

SOME GAMES

The grand master of chess, as recognized by the czar of Russia, Frank J. Marshall takes a minute to pose for the camera after defeating 17 Romans in chess. At the time of his 1922 visit, Marshall had already captured many honors in his career and reigned as the U.S. chess champion from 1909 to 1936.

Car races brought large crowds of spectators to the county fairgrounds, as shown in the above photograph taken around 1920. Two Romans appear on NASCAR's 50 Greatest Drivers of All Time list, Richie Evans and Jerry Cook. Evans won eight consecutive championships, from 1978 to 1985, before being killed in a crash in 1985. The number of his car, 61, has been retired from racing. (RHS.)

Flooding was a major concern in Rome with the vast amount of small waterways that ran throughout the city. A large concrete dam built in 1912 on the outskirts of Rome in the village of Delta was the solution. It took four years to build the dam. In the process, a portion of the village of Delta relocated and the remainder became submerged in what became Lake Delta. The water backfilled and flooded out surrounding areas, producing a very sizable scenic lake. Lake Delta remains a popular destination for boating, fishing, swimming, and picnicking at the New York State Park.

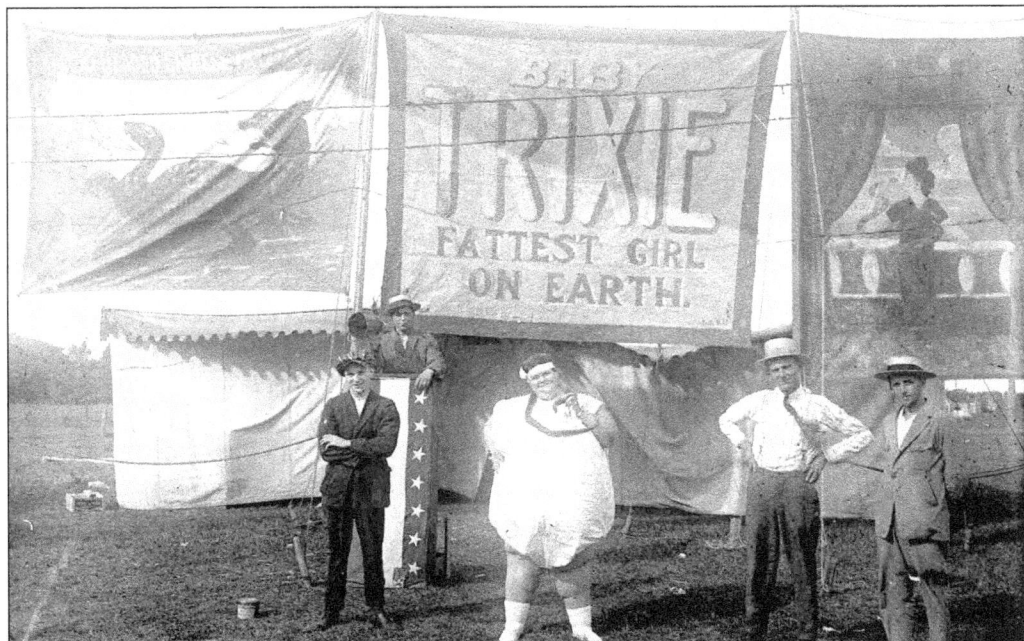

Traveling circuses and sideshows were a special treat when they came to town. Barking through the megaphone, the promoter is trying to arouse the curiosity of the crowd by tempting them with such oddities as Baby Trixie, the Fattest Girl on Earth, or the mythological creature known as the Two-Headed Chinese Pa-Lu-Ca.

All types of exhibits appeared at the county fair, from local businesses to agricultural products and displays. The main building of the county fair is shown in the above photograph. The county fairgrounds were located on upper Floyd Avenue. The first fair took place in 1841 and the last one in 1928.

The YMCA is one of Rome's oldest social clubs still in existence today. It began in 1871 and continued to grow in membership. Its first building on West Liberty Street was a welcome addition to the downtown area. The YMCA offered to the youth of Rome a chance to become involved in any number of sports teams and recreational programs it offered.

With the large number of manufacturing jobs in Rome came the need for union representation. Trade unions appeared throughout the city and for almost every trade imaginable. Shown above is the Mason's Union, the men that built Rome, literally. Also seen in the background is the Grogan Brothers tobacco shop at West Dominick Street.

Being involved in politics is another way of staying involved in the community. Rome has mostly swayed to the Republican Party since the election of Pres. Abraham Lincoln, who stopped in Rome in 1860. Huge banners stretched across Dominick Street advertising for the reelection of Pres. Benjamin Harrison in 1892. (RHS.)

Knights of the International Order of Good Templars are seen at a Christmas celebration held at the Rome YMCA in 1921. This particular fraternity had its beginnings in 1850 in Utica. Its belief system in total abstinence from alcoholic beverages allowed the organization to spread quickly worldwide.

The Rome Lodge No. 96 of the Benevolent and Protective Order of Elks now occupies the Wheeler Armstrong house at 126 West Liberty Street. Elkdom began in Rome in 1888 but did not see a resurgence in membership until the 1920s.

Even before the incorporation of the village of Rome in 1819, the Masonic fraternity was well established. Records dating back to 1799 document some of the first meetings of the Rome Lodge No. 223. Other allied Masonic lodges opened throughout the years, including Hathaway Lodge No. 869, Fort Stanwix Lodge No. 153, the Knights Templar Commandry No. 45, and the Order of the Eastern Star. Meetings and ceremonies took place at the temple on North Washington Street. Several Rome Masons are photographed below wearing their Masonic aprons and regalia. Many cornerstones of Rome's first and earliest buildings were laid with an elaborate Masonic ceremony.

The Independent Order of Odd Fellows Lodge No. 266 of Rome was photographed in front of its lodge at 120 West Liberty Street. The first lodge in the city began in 1844. Friendship, love, and truth were the principles of the fraternity.

The Boy Scout movement started in Rome when children of the First Baptist Church formed Troop No. 1 of the Rome Boy Scout Council. Several other Troops formed and then became part of the Fort Stanwix Council.

Rome had earned a respectable reputation for its two opera houses. Sink's Opera House held its first performance in 1869. A few years later, the Washington Street Opera House raised its curtain. A variety of operettas, dancers, orations, graduations, and vaudeville style shows graced the stages of these two houses. Both houses were lost to fire within a year of each other. In addition to stage performances, several movie theaters, like the Star, the Family Theater, the Strand, and the Casino, opened. The most elegantly designed movie theater was the Capitol Theatre. The above photograph shows the stage of the Washington Street Opera House, and the below photograph shows a dance troupe in action.

The Kallet family built the Capitol Theatre in the heart of downtown Rome. The marquee was an icon for many generations. The first movie *Lilac Time*, starring Gary Cooper, opened on December 10, 1928, to a sold-out crowd. As shown in the above and below photographs, large crowds of all ages of Romans would flock to the Capitol to watch the latest movie releases from Hollywood. Another treat was to stop next door at the Capitol Restaurant for an after-movie snack. The Capitol Theatre and the Capitol Restaurant closed in the 1970s and has since reopened as a center for performing arts and the occasional silent movie of yesteryear.

Eight

THAT ITALIAN TOUCH

The city of Rome can be considered an ethnic mixing pot. As the need for skilled labor increased so did the number of immigrants coming to Rome to seek employment. The early immigrants were mostly German, Polish, and Irish. The mass migration of Italians began in the 1890s. It was rumored in the 1930s that Italians outnumbered non-Italians three to one. Griffiss Air Force Base broadened the ethnicity of Rome even further. Wine cellars would almost certainly be found in an Italian household. It was here where the wine was brewed, and all types of sausages and cheeses were hung to dry, not to mention row upon row of home canned foods.

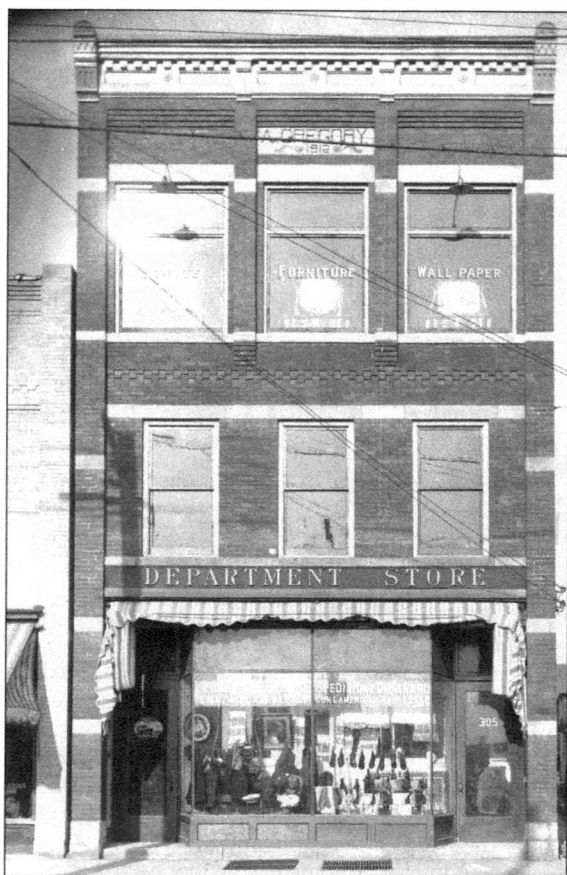

The Little Italy section of Rome was almost everything east of the Black River Canal. Most settled on River Street and areas along East Dominick Street because of the close proximity of the major factories like Revere, Rome Cable, Spargo Wire, and Rome Copper and Brass. On the right-hand side of the picture above is Rocco Gualtieri's Market, which also served as a branch of the Bank of Naples to its Italian patrons. The picture to the left shows the Gregory Block of East Dominick Street and the department store that was located there. The signage in the window also indicates that it sold more than household articles. Many of these stores were agents for shipping companies that arranged to bring loved ones from Italy to Rome or to send money back home for their families that were left behind.

Loggia Galliano No. 388 or the Galliano Club of Rome is an important men's social club. Organized in 1916, it has been an active part of the Rome community. It was named after Italian war hero Maj. Guiseppe Galliano, who died in battle engaged with the Ethiopian army in 1896. The photograph below shows the membership of the Galliano Club captured sometime in the 1960s. The club on East Dominick Street is complete with a bar, games of skill, bocce courts, and banquet facilities.

The Acme Club located on East Dominick Street opened in 1935. Membership was comprised mostly of high school and college students. The goal of the club was to promote friendship and social values through sports programs. They dominated the local sports scene in basketball and softball by the 1950s.

In 1925, the Protezione Toccolana di Benaficenza incorporated as the Toccolana Club. At first membership was exclusively reserved to those descending from that region of Italy, but it has now opened up membership to non-descendants. The 1950s-era membership of the club is pictured in the above photograph at 507 East Dominick Street.

Music was an important part of life for the Italians in Rome, and it seemed as if a member of every household played a musical instrument. As a result, several bands formed, like the Rome Italian Band shown in the above photograph. An event in East Rome could always rely on one thing: a brass band was always there!

Posing proudly in front of St. John the Baptist Church is the La Banda Bianco or the Rome White Band. The White Band was a well-known band in the area and a fixture at parades, funerals, and Catholic feasts. Following World War II, the White Band merged with the La Banda Rossa (the Red Band) in Utica and is still active at community events. (RHS.)

THE AGATHA PLAYERS

PRESENT . . . "Street Scene"
A 3 ACT PLAY
By ELMER RICE

☆

To Whom

This Program

is

Dedicated

☆

2nd LIEUT. ORLANDO FRANCIS DEL VECCHIO
1919 - 1944

COLUMBIAN HALL ☆ DECEMBER SEVENTEENTH ☆ 1944

Drawing on centuries of dramatic contributions, Agatha and Joseph Bottini left their mark in Rome by starting the East Rome Dramatic Club in 1919. Following Agatha's death in 1930, they renamed the company to the Agatha Players. Their plays, with the music of the White Band, would delight the crowds. The last stage performance took place in 1951. The program shown on the left features a former Agatha Player killed in World War II.

In 1971, the Italian societies of Rome adopted the program entitled A Vanishing Art. This wine-making float paraded down the streets of Rome to generate interest in the program. Many of the lifelong Italian residents of Rome felt the old traditions were being lost forever, and this was their way of preserving them.

116

Bocce is an Italian game of skill with origins back to the Roman Empire. Many variations of this game exist around the world. In 1973, a comment made by soon-to-be-mayor Carl Eilenberg lead to one of the most memorable sporting events in Rome's history, the World Series of Bocce. Seen at right, from left to right, (first row) Bobby DeSantis, and Cozy Costello; (second row) Tony Facciolo, Joe Taverna, and John DeProspero were the founding members and driving force behind this tournament. The first World Series of Bocce was held at the Kennedy Arena in 1974. As word spread, teams from around the world signed up to play. A special bocce pavilion was built behind the Rome Bowling Center where the next 21 World Series of Bocce tournaments were held. The members of the Toccolana Club now host the series, which is held every July.

On August 6, 1976, John DeProspero wanted to have a few friends over for dinner, so he set the table and put on the spaghetti. The table stretched the entire length of St. John the Baptist Church's parking lot. Known as "the Great Spaghetti Dinner of '76," it was actually an attempt to make the record books for the world's longest table. Many Romans turned out for the celebration, not too mention the pasta. Although meters short of the record, the profits were placed into trust and are now awarded as a scholarship to students of Italian American descent.

Nine

JUST BECAUSE

The creativity and ingenuity of Romans is what made Rome grow from a small little wilderness outpost into a heavily industrialized city that produced one-tenth of all cooper-related products in the United States. The lads pictured in the above photograph have decided to spend their spare time fishing in a mud puddle located next to city hall.

Many small upstate and western New York railroad ventures consolidated into the Rome, Watertown and Ogdensburg Railroad. Passengers nicknamed it "Rotten Wood and Old Rusty Rails." Expansions forced the company into bankruptcy, which led to its eventual merger with the New York Central Railroad in 1913. The old Rome passenger station on South James Street closed and then moved to its present location on Martin Street.

The first mode of transportation in Rome was the horse-drawn streetcar, inaugurated in 1887 as the Rome City Street Railway Company. Several cars were converted over to the Hardie Compressed Air Company's engines to power the cars. Eventually they were converted to a reliable electric engine. The streetcars became obsolete as more Romans began to own automobiles.

One cannot tell the history of Rome and not talk about the famous Upstate New York winters. Starting as early as September and ending as late as June, snow is a resident of the city. The yearly averages have declined, but usually Rome is blanketed with well over 100 or more inches of snowfall a year. In the photograph below, a city trolley car is struggling to make it up the small incline amid the towering banks of snow on all sides.

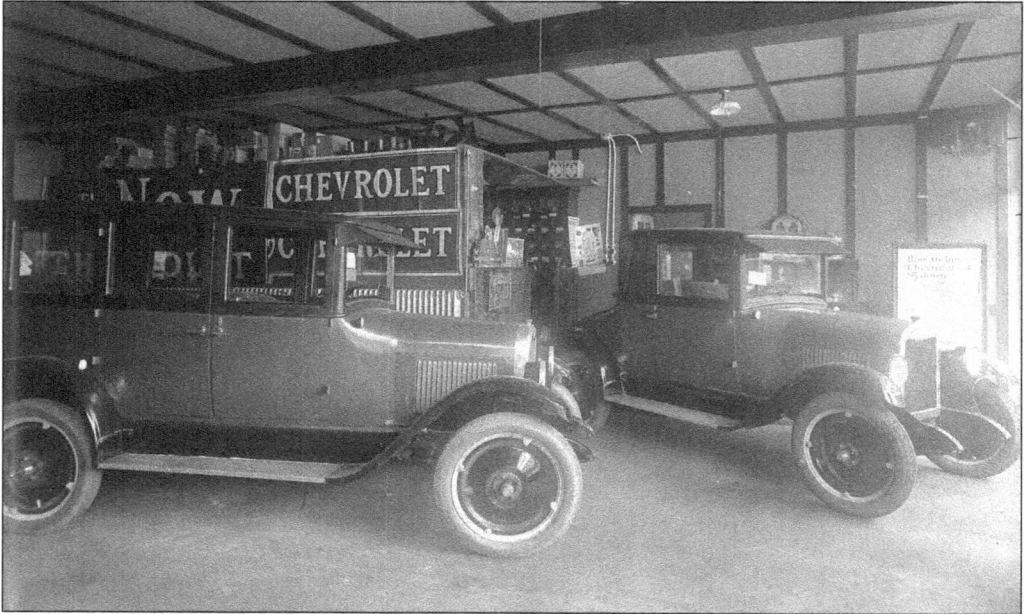

First came the invention of the automobile. This novelty machine was widely accepted throughout the city. Smith Brothers sold Ford and Woodruff Brothers sold Chevrolet brand automobiles. Several clubs and organizations formed to promote the growth of the automobile industry.

Next came the need for the gas station to provide the necessary fuel for the newly acquired automobile to run. Places like Sears and the Go-Gas stations opened all over the city to meet that demand. The Go-Gas station in the photograph above was located on James Street.

With the increased amount of automobiles traveling along city streets, the eventuality of the car accident became a reality. Although drivers were not allowed to travel faster than one mile in three minutes, the accident photographed above was most likely the result of speed and poor road conditions.

The mechanic and auto body repair shop became as important as the gas station. As gas stations refined their operations, many added mechanics and offered repairs to become the service station like Acchino's Shell Service and Body Works. Jerome and James Acchino started this station on Floyd Avenue in the 1950s.

With the 100th anniversary of the city of Rome approaching, the face of Rome was going to be changed forever. The city that was built on the ruins of Fort Stanwix and centralized around Dominick and James Streets contained many old and historic buildings. The rebirth of Fort Stanwix into a national park was the catalyst for citywide change. The nation engrossed itself in bicentennial fever, and the urban renewal movements tried to modernize everything that was old. This led to the razing of "old Rome." (RHS.)

Ancient buildings like the Empire House, the Stryker House, the Rome Club, the American Legion, the Arlington and Stanwix Hotels, and block after city block fell to the wrecking ball. Archaeologists then came in and began excavations at the site of what has now become Fort Stanwix National Monument.

Rome celebrated its 100th birthday as a city in 1970 with citywide celebrations. In the 150-plus years, Rome has been home to several noteworthy individuals. They include Francis Bellamy; Dr. Mary Walker and Maj. Oscar Burkhard, Congressional Medal of Honor winners; Wealthy Honsinger Fisher, humanitarian; Alex Haley and Harold Bell Wright, noted authors; Frederick Hodges, nature photographer; Jessie Williams, cheese maker; John B. Jervis, engineer; and numerous others.

Fort Stanwix National Monument is the most accurately reproduced fortress in North America right down to the locks and keys. Accuracy was made possible because the original maps and blueprints have survived through the years. Tens of thousands of visitors tour the fort and adjoining museum each year.

The archaeological team found the remains of several bodies just outside the fort walls on James Street. Forensic evidence showed they were all soldiers of the Revolutionary War period. Renowned architect Lorimer Rich designed a memorial tomb for these unknown soldiers. They were interred in copper caskets and buried at the corner of Liberty and James Streets in a small park that is now the Tomb of the Unknown Soldiers of the Revolutionary War.

The promoters of Woodstock were very impressed with the layout of Griffiss Air Force Base and the surrounding community. Rome was chosen to host Woodstock '99. Hundreds of thousands of concertgoers lined the two-and-a-quarter-mile runway and surrounding areas to listen to the music of their favorite groups. The concert provided a much-needed economic boost to the city.

All that remains of the famed American Corner is a brick outline of Fort Stanwix in the road. Much has changed since the time Dominick Lynch stood on this site and proclaimed this is Dominick Street, pivoted 90 degrees and proclaimed this is James Street. This is Rome, New York, the "City of American History."

Visit us at
arcadiapublishing.com

www.ingramcontent.com/pod-product-compliance
Lightning Source LLC
Chambersburg PA
CBHW050547110426
42813CB00008B/2277